SARA TEIDJ

Scientific computing by Matlab

SARA TEIDJ

Scientific computing by Matlab

Corrected courses and exercises

ScienciaScripts

Imprint
Any brand names and product names mentioned in this book are subject to trademark, brand or patent protection and are trademarks or registered trademarks of their respective holders. The use of brand names, product names, common names, trade names, product descriptions etc. even without a particular marking in this work is in no way to be construed to mean that such names may be regarded as unrestricted in respect of trademark and brand protection legislation and could thus be used by anyone.

Cover image: www.ingimage.com

This book is a translation from the original published under ISBN 978-620-2-54698-0.

Publisher:
Sciencia Scripts
is a trademark of
International Book Market Service Ltd., member of OmniScriptum Publishing Group
17 Meldrum Street, Beau Bassin 71504, Mauritius
Printed at: see last page
ISBN: 978-620-3-33459-3

Table of Contents

Introduction

This book is an introduction to Scientific Calculus. Its aim is to present numerical methods for solving mathematical problems with a computer that cannot be dealt with simply with a sheet of paper and a pen.

After the presentation of some basic *Matlab* elements, the main usual operations on scalars, vectors and matrices will be introduced. We will then see how to use script files (M-file) and functions with *Matlab* before presenting some graphic operations offered by this software.

In chapter 4 we will learn the syntax of the tests and the different programming loops in *Matlab*, and in chapter 5 we will see some of the more advanced functions existing in *Matlab*.

Finally, in chapters 6 we look at the application of numerical methods under *Matlab*:

It should be remembered here that a scientific language like *Matlab* requires rigour and perfect mastery.

Its apparent simplicity should not hide the effort required to learn the syntax it uses correctly and then to know how to translate mathematical algorithms into this language. A programming language cannot replace the upstream work of translating what you want to program into an algorithm and then into a flowchart.

Chapter 1: Introduction to the Matlab environment

1. Presentation of Matlab

Matlab is a programming language, but it is much more than that. It is in fact what is called an execution console (*shell*) which shares some of the characteristics of DOS or UNIX consoles.

Like all consoles, *Matlab* allows you to perform functions, assign values to variables, perform mathematical operations, manipulate matrices, easily draw graphs, etc.

Figure 1 shows the basic *Matlab* screen: the command window.

The >> symbol is called prompt or Matlab prompt. It prompts the user to type a command.

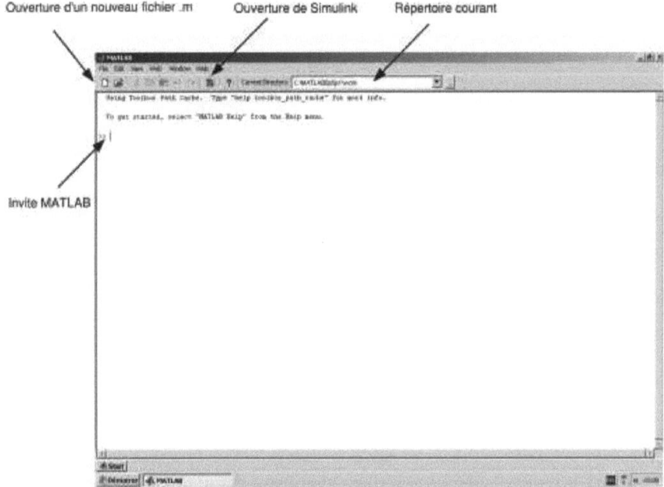

Figure 1: *Matlab* **command window**

The *quit* command exits MATLAB :
>> quit
The *help* command allows you to give help on a given problem.

It is worth noting that *Matlab* is not a compiled language (unlike C++, for example). It reads and executes programs instruction by instruction and line by line.

When *Matlab* detects an error, the software stops and an error message and the line where the error is detected are displayed on the screen. Learning how to read error messages is therefore important for "debugging" programmes quickly and efficiently.

2. Matlab's environment

Matlab displays several windows at startup. Depending on the version the following windows can be found:

Current Folder: indicates the current directory and the existing files.

Workspace: shows all existing variables with their types and values.

Command History: used to formulate our expressions and interact with Matlab. This is the window we use throughout this chapter.

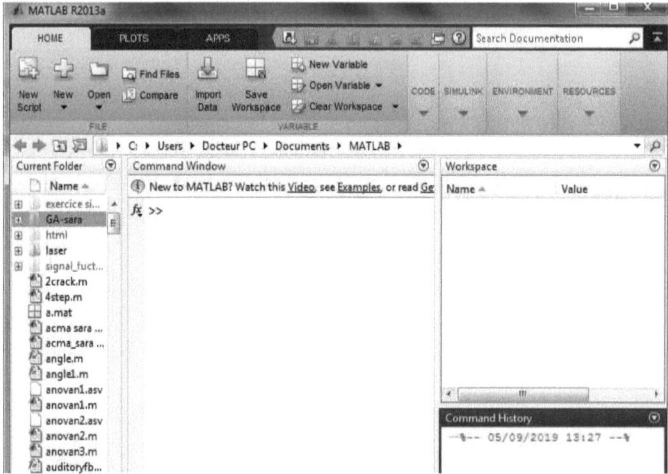

Figure 2: The *Matlab* environment

In the command window, the user can assign values to variables and perform operations on them.

For example :

> > x=4

x =

4

> > y=2

y =

2

> > x+y

years =

6
> > x*y
years =
8
>>
Here, it should be noted that when the user does not set an output variable, *Matlab* defaults the result of an operation to the *years* variable. It is always possible to know the variables used and their type using the *who* or *whos* command. For example, for previous operations:
> > whos

Name	Size	Byte s	Class
years	1x1 8	double	array
x	1x1 8	double	array
y	1x1 8	double	array

Grand total is 3 elements using 24 bytes
>>
The x+y solution was therefore lost. It is therefore preferable to always give names to the output variables :
> > x=4;
> > y=2;
> > a=x+y
a =
6
> > b=x*y
b=
8
> > whos

Name	Size	Byte s	Class
a	1x1 8	double	array
b	1x1 8	double	array
x	1x1 8	double	array
y	1x1 8	double	array

Grand total is 4 elements using 32 bytes
>>
It should be noted in passing that the semicolon makes it possible not to show afficher the value on the screen, which will eventually allow faster programmes.
The percentage sign (%) is used to put the following on a line as a comment (*Matlab* will ignore it at runtime).
The *clear* function allows effacer variables. For example :

> > clear x % on   erase x from memory
> > whos

Name	Size	Bytes	Class
a	1x1 8	double	array
b	1x1 8	double	array
y	1x1 8	double	array

Grand total is 3 elements using 24 bytes
>>

The output of the *whos* function gives, among other things, the class of the variable. Several classes of variables are available to the *Matlab* user.

The percentage sign % allows you to put the following on a line as a comment (Matlab will not take it into account at runtime).

The most useful classes for the novice user are integer, single real, double real and char variables.

 For *char* variables, the statement is made between apostrophes:

word1 = 'hello' > > word2 = 'hello' > word3 = 'hello' > word4 = 'hello

word1 = hello

It is possible to concatenate words using square brackets (the *Matlab strcat* function allows you to perform much the same task):

> > word1 = 'hello';

> word2 = 'everyone';

> > word1_2 = [word1 ' ' word2] % using ' ' allows you to enter a space

mot1_2 = hello everyone.

3. The main constants, functions and controls

Matlab defines the following constants:

The constant	Its value
pi	$\pi=3.1415.....$
exp(1)	$e=2.7183$
i	$=\sqrt{-1}$
j	$=\sqrt{-1}$
Inf	∞
NaN	Not a Number
eps	$\varepsilon\approx 2\times 10^{-16}$

Frequently used functions include the following:

The function	Its significance
sin(x)	The sinus of x (in radian)

cos(x)	The cosine of x (in radian)
tan(x)	The tangent of x (in radian)
asin(x)	The sine arc of x (in radian)
acos(x)	The cosine arc of x (in radian)
atan(x)	The tangent arc of x (in radian)
sqrt(x)	The square root of x : $\sqrt{x}$
abs(x)	The absolute value of x : $\|x\|$
exp(x)	$=e^x$
log(s)	Natural logarithm of x : $\ln(x)=\log_e(x)$
log10(x)	Logarithm based on 10 of x : $\log_{10}(x)$
imag(s)	The imaginary part of the complex number x
real(s)	The real part of the complex number x
round(s)	Rounding a number to the nearest integer
floor(s)	Round a number to the smallest integer: $\max\{n\|n\leq x, n\,entier\}$
ceil(s)	Round a number to the largest integer: $\max\{n\|n\geq x, n\,entier\}$
conj(X)	conjugate of the complex number X
angle(X)	argument (in radians)

Matlab offers a lot of controls for user interaction. For the time being we are content with a small set, and we will expose the others as the course progresses.

The order	Its significance
who	Displays the name of the variables used
whos	Displays information on the variables used
clear x y	Removes the variables x and y
clear, clear all	Deletes all variables
clc	Clears the screen
exit,quit	Close the Matlab environment
format: long format format short e long format e	Sets the output format for numeric values. long format with 15 digits. Short 5-digit format with floating point notation. 15-digit long format with floating point notation.
disp	allows you to display a table of numeric values or characters.
Num2str	to convert a numeric value into a string of characters
Input	allows you to ask the user of a program to provide data (The syntax is var = input (' a sentence ').

Chapter 2: Basic mathematical operations with *Matlab:*

Scales, vectors and matrices

Several types of data are available in *Matlab*. The traditional types found in all programming languages: numeric types (single, double, int8, etc...), char characters, real arrays, and sparse arrays, and cell, structure and user defined types, such as *inline* functions. The preferred data type under *Matlab* is one- or two-dimensional tables, which correspond to the vectors and matrices used in mathematics and which are also used for graphical representation. We will therefore focus on their definition and handling in the following paragraphs.

The basic element of *Matlab* is the matrix. I.e. a scalar is a matrix of dimension 1x1, a column vector of dimension n is a matrix nx1, a row vector of dimension n, a matrix 1xn. Contrary to common programming languages (i.e. C++), it is not mandatory to declare variables before using them and, therefore, all precautions must be taken in the handling of these objects.

Scalars declare themselves directly, for example :

> > x = 0;

> > a = x;

1. Vectors

Line vectors are declared as follows:

V_line   = [0 1 2] >> V_line = [0 1 2

V_line =

0   1   2

Or

V_line = [0, 1, 2] >> V_line = [0, 1, 2

V_line =

   0   1   2

For column vectors, the elements are separated by semicolons (;):

V_column   = [0;1;2] >> V_column = [0;1;2

V_column =

0

1

2

A vector can be transposed using the *transpose* function or with the apostrophe point (. '). Thus,

>> V_column=transpose   (V_line)
V_column =
0
1
2
>> V_column=V_line   .'
V_column =
0
1
2
The colon (:) is the increment operator in *Matlab*. Thus, to create a line vector of values from 0 to 1 in increments of 0.2, simply use:
> > V= [0:0.2:1]
V =
Columns 1 through 6
0   0.2000   0.4000   0.6000   0.8000   1.0000
By default, the increment is 1, so to create a line vector of values from 0 to 5 in increments of 1, simply use :
> > V=[0:5]
V =
0   1   2   3   4   5
One can access an element of a vector and even modify it directly (Note that unlike C++, there is **no index 0** in vectors and matrices in *Matlab*) :
> > a=V(2);
> > V(3)=3*a
V =
0   1   3   3   4   5
The creation of a vector whose components are ordered at regular intervals and with a specific number of elements can be done with the *linspace* function (start, end, number of elements).
The increment step is calculated automatically by Matlab according to the following formula:

$$le\ pas = \frac{fin - début}{nombre\ d'éléments - 1}$$

>> X=space(1,10,4) % a vector of four elements from 1 to 10
X =
    1   4   7   10
The size of a vector (the number of its components) can be obtained with the *length* function as follows:

\>> length(X) % the   size of the X vector
years =
     4
The usual addition, subtraction and scalar multiplication operations on vectors
are defined in MATLAB :
\> > V1=[1 2];
\> > V2=[3 4];

\> > V=V1+V2 % addition of vectors
V =
4   6
\> > V=V2-V1 % vector subtraction
V =
2   2
\> > V=2*V1 %   multiplication by a scalar
V =
2   4
In the case of multiplication and division, attention must be paid to the
dimensions of the vectors involved.
For multiplication and division element by element, a dot is added in front of the
operator (.* and ./). For example, a point is added in front of the operator (.*
and ./):
\> V=V1.*V2 %   multiplication element by element

V =
3   8
\> V=V1./V2 %   division element by element
V =
0.3333   0.5000
However, *Matlab* throws an error when the dimensions do not match. Error
messages are useful for correcting programmes (e.g. forgotten parenthesis).
However, it is necessary to systematically check the instruction or programme
before starting the execution (basic reflex of a programmer):
\> > V3=[1 2 3]
V3 =
1   2   3
\> > V=V1.*V3
??? Error using ==> .* Matrix dimensions must agree.
The multiplication of two vectors is given by (*). Here, the order is important:

\> > V1=[1 2]; % vector 1x2
\> > V2=V1.'; % vector   2x1
\> > V=V1*V2
V =
5
\> > V=V2*V1
V =
1   2
2   4
It is also possible to concatenate vectors.
 For example :
\> > V1=[1 2];
\> > V2=[3 4];
\> > V=[V1 V2].
V =
1   2   3   4
Similarly, for column vectors :
\> > V1=[1;2];
\> > V2=[3;4];
\> > V=[V1;V2].
V =
1
2
3
4

2. Matrixes

Matrices can also be created from vectors, for example,
\> > V1=[1 2];
\> > V2=[3 4];
\> > V=[V1;V2].
V =
1   2
3   4
which is not equivalent to :
\> > V1=[1;2];
\> > V2=[3;4];
\> > V=[V1 V2].

V =

| 1 | 3 |
| 2 | 4 |

It is therefore necessary to be very careful when handling vectors. For example, poor concatenation :

> > V1=[1 2];
> > V2=[3;4];
> > V=[V1;V2].

??? Error using ==> vertcat All rows in the bracketed expression must have the same number of columns.

The matrices can also be constructed directly :

> > M=[1 2; 3 4]

M =

| 1 | 2 |
| 3 | 4 |

The elements of the matrix can of course be accessed by :

>> m21=M(2.1) % 2nd   row, 1st column

m21 =

3

You can also "count" the elements. *Matlab* then counts all the elements in a column (from top to bottom) before moving on to the next column. Thus, in the following 3x3 matrix:

> > A=[1 2 3; 8 5 6;7 8 9]

A =

1	2	3
8	5	6
7	8	9

The values of the elements ai,j are given by their rank assigned by *Matlab*. The4th element is 2 :

> > a4=A(4)

a4 =

2

It is also possible to store one or more rows (or columns) in a vector. Thus, if one wants to store the second column of the matrix A :

> V=A(:,2) % here,   (:) means all lines

V =

2
5
8

In the same way, if you want to store lines 2 and 3 :
> > M2=A(2:3,:) % (2:3   ) means line 2 to 3
% and (:) means all columns
M2 =
8   5   6
7   8   9
It is possible to invert *inv*(), transpose *transpose*() or with the apostrophe (. ') the matrices :
> > invM=inv(M)
invM =
-2.0000   1.0000
1.5000   -0.5000
> > transpM=M. '
transpM =
1   3
2   4
One of the interests of *Matlab* is the possibility to directly use predefined mathematical operations for matrices. Addition and subtraction are direct (pay attention to the dimensions) as well as multiplication by a scalar :
> > A=[1 2;3 4];
> > B=[4 3;2 1];
> > C=A+B % addition
C=
5   5
5   5
> > D=A-B % subtraction
D=
-3   -1
1   3
> > C=3*A % multiplication by a scalar
C=
3   6
9   12
The usual operators (* and /) are defined for matrix multiplication and division :
> > C=A*B % matrix   multiplication
C=
8   5
20   13
> > D=A/B % matrix   division

D=

1.5000   -2.5000

2.5000   -3.5000

In order to carry out the multiplication and division element by element, the operators are preceded by a dot (.* and ./) :

> C=A.*B %   multiplication element by element

C=

4   6

6   4

> D=A./B %   division element by element

D=

0.2500   0.6667

1.5000   4.0000

Further operations on the matrices will be presented in subsequent sections.

It is important to note some special matrices that can be used, for example the identity matrix :

> > I=eye(3) % identity matrix

I=

1   0   0

0   1   0

0   0   1

Vectors (and matrices) containing only zeros or 1s can also be declared.

> V_nul=zeros(1,2) % a vector of 1 line, 2 columns of 0

V_nul=

0   0

> V_un=ones(1,2) % a vector of 1 row, 2 columns of 1

V_un=

1   1

> > M_un=ones(2,2) % a 2x2 matrix of 1

M_un=

1   1

1   1

In some applications, it is sometimes useful to know the dimensions of a matrix, and the length of a vector (returned, for example, by a function).

In this case, the *length* and *size* functions are used.

> > V=[0:0.1:10]; % length use - vector 1x101

> > n=length(V)

n=

101
> M=[1 2 3; 4 5 6]; % use of size - 2x3 matrix
> > [n,m]=size(M)
n=
2
m=
3
> > dim=length(M) %   use of length on a die
Sun=
3
In this case *length* gives the largest dimension, here the number of columns.

A=[1 2 3 ; 2 4 5 ; 6 7 8];
det(A) % calculates the determinant of A
>> det(A)
years =
   -5.0000
>> B=[-5 -2; 2 1];
>> abs(B) % the absolute   value
years =
    5   2
    2   1
There are also commands that are specific to vectors, and these commands also apply to matrices. In this case the command is for each column vector of the matrix.

The order	Its significance
sum(x)	Sum of the elements of vector x
prod(x)	produces elements of the x-vector
max(x)	largest element of the x-vector
min(x)	smallest element of vector x
mean(x)	mean of the elements of the vector x
spell(s)	arranges the elements of the x-vector in ascending order

3. Polynomials in Matlab

In Matlab, polynomials are represented as line vectors whose components are given in order of decreasing power. A polynomial of degree n is represented by a size vector (n+1).

   a) Representation of a polynomial

The polynomial: p(x)=3x² - 5x + 2

We start by defining a "vector" which contains the coefficients of the polynomial :

p = [3 -5 2]

p =

   3   -5   2

b) The roots of a polynomial:

The *roots* function is used to find the roots of a polynomial. The following example shows the use of this function.

roots(p) % find the roots of a polynomial

years =

1.0000

0.6667

c) Determination of the coefficients of a polynomial from its roots

The *poly* function allows you to find the polynomial from its roots.

 For example, we are looking for the polynomial with roots: 2 and 1.

These can be defined as the elements of a vector a.

a=[2 1]

a =

   2   1

>> poly(a) %find the polynomial from its roots

years =

   1   -3   2

Which corresponds to   f(x)= x² -3x +2

d) Evaluating the polynomial

To evaluate a polynomial at one point, the *polyval* function

Let's try to find the value of the polynomial p in 1 and that of the polynomial a in 0.

>> p = [3 -5 2]

p =

   3   -5   2

>> polyvalent(p,1) %   evaluates the polynomial

years =

   0

>> a=[2 1]

a =

   2   1

>> versatile(a,0)

years =
        1

e) Polynomial operations

Multiplication and division of polynomials can be easily performed with MATLAB. Let two polynomials P1 and P2 defined by :

$P1(x)=x+2$

$P2(x)=x^2-2x+1$

```
>> P1=[1 2]
P1 =
     1    2
>> P2=[1 -2 1]
P2 =
     1   -2    1
```

The result of multiplying P1 by P2 is the polynomial P3 which is obtained with the function *conv*.

```
>> P3=conv(P1,P2)
P3 =
     1    0   -3    2
```

The division of two polynomials is done by the *deconv* function. The quotient Q and the remainder R of the division can be obtained as part of a table.

```
>> [Q, R] = deconv (P2, P1)
Q =
     1 -  4
R =
     0    0    9
```

4. Extraction of a sub-matrix

The two dots can be used to extract a sub-matrix from an A-matrix.

A(:,j) :extracts the jth column of A. We consider successively all the lines of A and choose the jth element of each line.

A(i,:):extracts the ith line of A.

A(:) :reformats the matrix A into a single column vector by concatenating all the columns of A.

A(j:k) :extracts elements j to k from A and stores them in a line vector

A(:,j:k) :extracts the sub-matrix of A formed from columns j to k.

A(j:k,:): extracts the submatrix of A formed from lines j to k.

A(j:k,q:r) :extracts the sub-matrix of A formed from the elements located in the rows j to ket in the columns q to r.

These definitions can be extended to incremental steps of the rows and columns different from 1.

For example:
>> A=[1 2 3 4; 5 6 7 8;9 10 11 12] %   creation of matrix A
A =
     1   2   3   4
     5   6   7   8
     9   10   11   12
>> A(2.3) % of the element in the 2nd row to the 3rd column
years =
     7
>> A(1,:) % all   elements of the 1st line
years =
     1   2   3   4
>> A(:,2) % all   elements of the 2nd column
years =
     2
     6
    10
>> A(2:3,:) % all   elements of the 2nd and 3rd line
years =
     5   6   7   8
     9   10   11   12
>> A(1:2,3:4) % the upper right sub-matrix size 2x2
years =
     3   4
     7   8
>> A([1.3],[2.4]) % per   sub-matrix: row (1.3) and columns (2.4)
years =
     2   4
    10   12
>> A(:,3)=[] %   delete 3rd column
A =
     1   2   4
     5   6   8
     9   10   12
>> A(2,:)=[] %   delete 2nd line
A =

```
   1    2    4
   9   10   12
>> A=[A , [0;0]] % Add a new column or A(:,4)=[0;0]
A =
   1    2    4    0
   9   10   12    0
>> A= [A ; [1, 1, 1]] % Add a new line or A(3,:)= [1 1 1 1 1] % Add a new line
or A(3,:)= [1 1 1 1 1] % Add a new line or A(3,:)= [1 1 1 1 1
A =
   1    2    4    0
   9   10   12    0
   1   1 1    1
```

5. Automatic matrix generation:

In Matlab, there are functions that allow the automatic generation of particular matrices. In the following table we present the most used ones:

The function	Meaning
zeros(n)	Generates an nxn matrix with all elements=0
zeros(m,n)	Generates an mxn matrix with all elements=0
ones(n)	Generates an nxn matrix with all elements=1
ones(m,n)	Generates an mxn matrix with all elements=1
eye(n)	Generates an identity matrix of dimension nxn
magic(n)	Generates a magical matrix of nxn dimension
rand(m,n)	Generates a matrix dimension mxn of random value

Chapter 3: *Script* and *function* files

So far, our use of *Matlab is* very similar to that of a calculator. For repetitive tasks, it is much more practical and judicious to write programs to perform the desired calculations.

There are two types of files that can be programmed with *Matlab*: *script* files (M-file) and *function* files. In both cases, the file editor has to be started and the file has to be saved with the extension **. m**.

1. *Script* files

Like any language, *Matlab* also has a certain number of syntactic instructions (simple loops, conditional, etc...) and elementary commands (reading, writing, etc...). These syntactic instructions will be seen in the next part of the course.

As soon as the calculation to be carried out involves a somewhat complicated sequence of commands, it is best to write these to a file. By convention a file containing *Matlab* commands has a name with the suffix **.m and** is therefore called an ***M-file*** or *script*. You will **always** use **the editor integrated in the software** which is launched from the command window by clicking on the **New** or **open** icons in the menu bar.

An editing window like this one will appear:

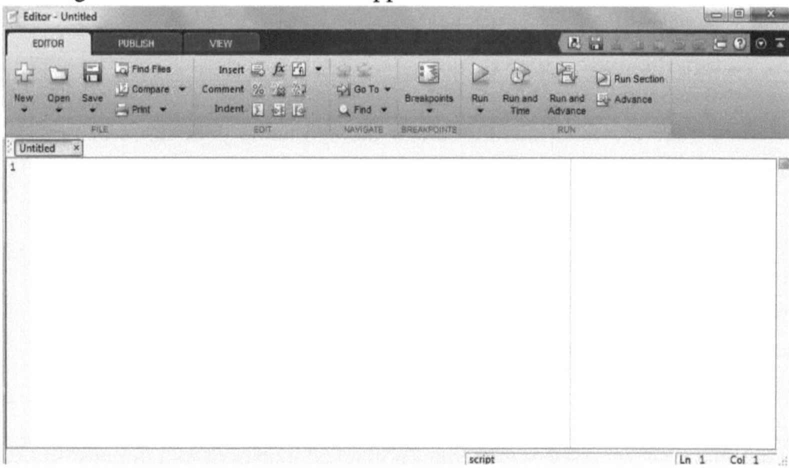

Figure 3: The *Matlab* editing window

Once the file has been saved with a valid name, you can execute the commands it contains by typing its name - without the .m suffix - in the command window. If you have opened the editor as indicated, from the command window, the M-file will be created in the current directory, accessible from this window, and you will have no access problems. If you want to run scripts that are located elsewhere in the file tree, you may have to change the *Path* by clicking on the menu **file- > SetPath or** by changing the working directory (click on the **current directory** tab).

The *script* file allows you to launch the same operations as those written directly to the *Matlab* command window after the prompt symbol (>>). All variables used in a *script* are available at the *Matlab* prompt (command windows) once the script is executed.

A *Matlab* script consists of a sequence of instructions, all separated by a comma (or equivalently, a line break) or a semicolon. The difference between these two types of separation is related to whether or not the result is displayed on the screen (only in the first case).

For example, let's create using the integrated *Matlab* editor in the chosen working directory, already declared by SetPath, the test.m file. Suppose it contains the following instructions:

clear all

close all

x=4;

y=2;

a=x +y

b=x*y

Let us write in the command window the name of the file

> > test

a =

6

b =

8

By typing *whos* next, the next output is produced:

Name	Size	Bytes	Class	
a	1x1 8	double	array	
b	1x1 8	double	array	
x	1x1 8	double	array	
y	1x1 8	double	array	

Grand total is 4 elements using 32 bytes

>>

Usually, *script* files are used to :

- Declaring variables ;
- Perform mathematical operations ;
- Calling up functions ;
- Drawing figures ;
- Programming algorithms.

2. Files *function* (M-file function)

The basic idea of a function is to perform operations on one or more inputs or arguments to obtain a result that will be called an output. It is worth noting that the function is called by specifying its input variables if these are not available at the *Matlab* prompt.

It is possible to create our own functions by writing their "source" codes in M-files (with the same function name) using the following syntax:

function $[r_1, r_2, ,...., r_n]$ = function_name ($arg_1, , ,..., arg_2 \; arg_n$)

        % the body of the function

r_1 = % the value returned for r_1

r_2 = % the value returned for r_2

r_n = % the value returned for r_n

% end is optional

end

where : $r_1, r_2, , ..., r_n$ are the returned values , and $arg_1, arg_2, , , ..., arg_n$ are the arguments.

the role of a function is to perform operations on one or more inputs to obtain a result that will be called output.

For example, the following function admits a single output a which is the result of adding the two input arguments x and y:

function a = my_function(x,y)

a=x+y;

end

When typing in the command window:

> > a = my_function(4,2)

you get

a = 6

Next, we check that

> > whos

Name   Size   Byte   s   Class

a   1x1 8   double   array

Grand total is 1 element using 8 bytes

>>

Let's modify the function to ask it to also calculate the product of x and y in the following way:

function [a,b] = my_function2(x,y)

a=x+y;

b=x*y;

end

In this case, we check that:

> > [a,b] = my_function2(4,2)

a =
6
b =
8
> > whos
Name   Size   Byte s   Class
a   1x1 8   double   array
b   1x1 8   double   array
Grand total is 2 elements using 16 bytes
>>
The display of outputs can be avoided by using the semicolon :
> > [a,b]=my_function2(4,2);
> > whos
Name   Size   Byte s   Class
a   1x1 8   double   array
b   1x1 8   double   array
Grand total is 2 elements using 16 bytes
Note that we can call the function my_function2 to calculate only the sum of x
and y. We then obtain
> > a = my_function2(4,2)
a =
6
> > whos
Name   Size   Byte s   Class
a   1x1 8   double   array
Grand total is 1 element using 8 bytes

Important notes :
* Input arguments in functions are passed by value. Therefore, even if they are
changed in the function, the parameter values are not changed in the calling
program.
* If one of the variables of the procedure is not defined within the procedure, it
must be provided as an input argument.
* The values calculated by the function are retrieved by the output parameters.
* The name of the file containing the function must be the name of the function.
Several functions can be put in the same M-file, but only the function with the
same name as the file can be used, called, from the command window or from
another function or script. Any other functions that may be stored in the file can
be called together but are not visible from the outside.

Usually the *function* files afin from :
- Programming repetitive operations ;
- Limit the number of variables in the *Matlab* prompt ;
- Divide the programme (problem) clearly.

3. Defining a function using the "*inline*" command

A function with only a small number of instructions can be defined directly in the command window as follows:
>>angle=inline('atan(y/x)')
angle = angle = angle = angle = angle = angle = angle = angle = angle = angle = angle = angle
Inline function:
angle(x,y) = atan(y/x)
>> angle(5,4)
years   =
0.6747
The arguments of the angle function are normally provided to the caller in the order of appearance in the function definition. Alternatively, call arguments can be specified explicitly
>>f =inline('sin(alpha*(x+y))', 'x', 'y', 'alpha')
f =
Inline function:
f(x,y,alpha) =sin(alpha*(x+y))
>>f(0.2,0.3,ft)
years =
1
4. Tool functions

Finally, note that some special commands can only be used in relation to a function: *nargin*, gives the number of input arguments passed when the function is called.
function c=testarg1(a,b)
if (nargin == 1)
c=2*a;
elseif (nargin == 2)
c=a+b;
end
nargin can also be used to find out the expected number of input arguments.

> > nargin('testarg1')
years =
2
The *nargout* command works in a similar way for output arguments.

Chapter 4: Functions and graphical representation in *Matlab*

1. Simple graphics

This section is an introduction to the many graphic faculties offered by *Matlab*.
In all graphical representations, the software is based on discrete data arranged in matrices or column vectors. For example, to represent curves of the type y = f(x) or areas z = f(x, y), the x, y, z data must be column vectors (x and y) or matrices (z) with compatible dimensions. The corresponding drawing instruction (e.g. plot(x,y) for drawing flat curves) is then used and possibly supplemented with optional arguments (colour, line type, scale on axes, etc.). The result is displayed in a graphical window (with the possibility of zooming, rotating, printing).

a) *The plot function:*
The **plot** function can be used with vectors or matrices. It draws lines by connecting coordinate points defined in its arguments, and it has several shapes:
If it contains two vectors of the same size as arguments: it considers the values of the first vector as the elements of the X-axis (the abscissae), and the values of the second vector as the elements of the Y-axis (the ordinate), as in the following example:
>> A=[2 5 3 -2 0]
A =
   2   5   3   -2   0
>> B=[-4 0 3 1 4]
B =
   -4   0   3   1   4
       >> plot(A,B)
If it contains a single vector as an argument: it considers the values of the vector as elements of the Y-axis (the ordinates), and their relative positions will define the X-axis (the abscissae),
Example:1
>> V=[2 1 6 8 -3 0 5]
V =

2   1   6   8   -3   0   5
>> plot(V)
>>
Example:2
> > x=[0:0.01:2*pi];
> > plot(x,cos(x))

b) *Changing the appearance of a curve*

However, these graphs lack clarity. It is possible to manipulate the appearance of a curve by changing the colour of the curve, the shape of the coordinate points and the type of line connecting the points.

This is done by adding a new argument (which can be called a marker) of string type to the *plot* function like this:

plot(x,y,' marker')

The content of the marker is a combination of a set of special characters collected in the following spreadsheet:

Colour of the curve		Representation of points	
The character	Its effect	-	In full line
b	Curve in blue	:	Dotted line
g	Green curve	--	In dashes
r	Curve in red	.	One point
y	Curve in yellow	o	A circle
k	Curve in black	x	The x symbol

To find out more, especially about colours and types of curves, typehelp *plot* at the *Matlab* prompt.

c) *Annotation of a figure:*

In a figure, it is preferable to put a textual description to help the user to understand the meaning of the axes and to know the purpose or interest of the visualisation concerned.

It is also very interesting to be able to indicate significant locations or points in a figure with a commentary indicating their importance.

✓ To give a title to a figure containing a curve we use the *title* function like this:

>> title (' figure title')

✓ To give a title for the vertical y-axis, we use the *ylabel* function like this:

>> ylabel(' this is the Y-axis ')

✓ To give a title for the horizontal x-axis, we use the *xlabel* function like this:

>> xlabel(' this is the X-axis ')

✓ To write text (a message) on the graphics window at a position indicated by the x and y coordinates, we use the *text* function like this:

>> text(x,y, 'this point is important')

✓ To put a text on a position chosen manually by the mouse, we use the *gtext* function, which has the following syntax:

>> gtext('this point is chosen manually')

✓ To put in a grid (a grid) we use the *grid on* command and to remove it we use the same *grid off* command.

✓ To set the limits on the abscissa and ordinate axes

>> axis([xmin xmax ymin ymax])

For example:

Let's draw the function: $y=-2x^3+x^2-2x+4$ for x varying from -4 to 4, with a 0.5 step.

clear all
close all
x=-4:0.5:4;
y=-2.*x.^3+x.^2-2.*x+4;
plot(x,y)
grid on
title(' Draw a curve')
xlabel('The abscissa axis')
ylabel('The ordinate axis')

d) Display several curves in the same window (hold on)

It is possible to display several curves in the same graphical window using the *hold on* command. The results of all graphic instructions executed after calling the *hold on command* will be superimposed on the active graphic window. To restore the previous situation (the result of a new graphic instruction replaces the previous drawing in the graphics window), press *hold off*.

Here is an example of how to use the *hold on* command

clear all
close all
x=space(0,ft,30);
y1=cos(x);
plot(x,y1,'o-r')
y2=sin(x);

```
hold on
plot(x,y2,'x-b')
y3=exp(-x);
hold on
plot(x,y3,'*-g')
```

e) Use plot with several arguments.

One can use plot with several couples (x,y) or triplets (x,y,' marker') as arguments. A script is very suitable:

```
% graph.m
clear all
close all
x=[0:0.01:2*pi];
y1=cos(x); y2=sin(x);
figure(1)
plot(x,y1,'.',x,y2,'+')            % cos(x) in points . , sin(x) in +
title('sine and cosine')
xlabel('x')
 ylabel('f(x)')
legend('cos(x)', 'sin(x)',0)       % the 0 places the legend next to the curves
```

Remark

There are therefore two ways of superimposing several curves on the same figure.

You can either give several pairs of absciss/ordinate vectors as an argument to the plot command, or use the *hold on* command. Depending on the context, one of these solutions will be preferred over the other.

2. Display multiple graphics (subplot)

This is a very useful feature for presenting a large number of results on the same graphic page.

The general idea is to cut the graphics window into blocks of the same size, and to display a graph in each block. The *subplot* instruction is used, specifying the number of blocks in height, the number of blocks in width, and the number of the block to be plotted in:

subplot (Number of paving stones on height, Number of paving stones on width, Number of paving stones)

The comma can be omitted. The keypads are numbered in the reading direction of a text: from left to right and from top to bottom.

Once a *subplot* command is typed, all subsequent graphic commands will be executed in the specified pad.

As an example, type the following sequence of instructions:

clear all

close all

x=[0:0.01:2*pi];

subplot(221)

plot(x,sin(x),'b')

subplot(222)

plot(x,cos(x),'r')

subplot(223)

plot(cos(2*x), 'g')

subplot(224)

plot(sin(2*x), 'k')

3. Logarithmic scales

Log scales can be drawn on the abscissa, ordinate or both. The corresponding functions are called *semilogx, semilogy* and *loglog* respectively. They are used in exactly the same way as *plot*.

For example :

>> x=1:100;

>> semilogx(x,log(x))

4. Other types of representation

In addition to the Cartesian representation of curves or surfaces, there are other possibilities to graphically illustrate a result. Among the most useful are *contour* instructions, *ezmesh* (for drawing *contour* lines of a parametric surface), *mesh,ezplot3* (parametric curves in space),*hist, rose* (histogram of a sample of statistical data), etc...

Type	Description	order
semilogy	y-axis in base log 10 and linear x-axis	semilogy(x,y)
semilogx	log x-axis and linear y-axis	semilogx(x,f(x))
loglog	both axes are in basic log 10	loglog(x,y)

errorbar	graph with error bar in y on each value	errorbar(x,y,e);
		 e: error vector at each point of x.
		 errorbar(x,y,eup,^{edown});
		 eup: being the upper limit of the error and ^{edown} the lower limit.

bar barh	graphic with vertical or horizontal bars	bar(x,y) barh(x,y)
hist	histogram	hist(y,nbins); nbins = no. of bars hist(y,x); x = location of the centre of the bar
plot3	Drawing of a parametric line in 3D	plot3(x,y,z)
mesh	Drawing of a 3D surface from mesh matrices	mesh(x,y,z)
surf	Drawing of a 3D surface with colour gradient from mesh matrices	surf(x,y,z)

5. Simple mathematical functions

The algebraic operators (+, -, *, /, . *, ./) have been previously defined for scalars, vectors and matrices. We will show here (without being exhaustive), the main mathematical functions provided in *Matlab* and their use. For functions not shown, the user can always use the help function with the *help function* taking the name of the function as argument. For example, the cosine function:

> > help cos

COS   Cosine of argument in radians.

COS(X) is the cosine of the elements of X.

In the following, the usual mathematical functions and their use in *Matlab* are presented. Next, the main functions specific to matrices are presented.

6. Usual mathematical functions

All the basic mathematical functions are already programmed in *Matlab*.

All common and less common functions are available. Most of them operate **in a complex**. To apply a function to a value, the value must be put in brackets. For example, to apply a function to a value, the value must be put in brackets:

>> sin(pi/12)

years =

0.165896132693 42

Here is a non-exhaustive list:

- trigonometric and inverse functions: sin, cos, tan, asin, acos, atan
- hyperbolic functions (add "h"): sinh, cosh, tanh, asinh, acosh, atanh
- root, logarithms and exponentials: sqrt, log, log10, exp
- error functions: erf, erfc
- Bessel and Hankel functions: besselj, bessely, besseli, besselk, besselh and hankel. Two parameters are needed: the order of the function and the argument itself. Thus J1(3) will be written besselj(1,3)

The notion of function is more general in *Matlab*, and some functions can have several inputs (like besselj for example) but also several outputs.

a) Matrix functions

All basic matrix functions are already programmed in *Matlab*.

Here are a few examples:

Size, length, diag, det, norm, rank, trace, sum, prod, mean, std, var, max, min, rand, null, inv, pinv, sort, reshape, fliplr, flipud, tril, triu,...

b) Advanced functions

These are functions that intervene in numerical analysis such as: lu, chol, qr, cond, eig, fzero,...

Chapter 5: Programming with *Matlab* and control structures

So far we have seen how to use *Matlab to* perform commands or to evaluate expressions by writing them in the command line, so the commands used are usually written as a single instruction (possibly on a single line).

However, there are problems where the description of their solutions requires several instructions, which in turn requires the use of several lines. For example, the search for the roots of a second-degree equation (taking into account all possible cases). A collection of well-structured instructions to solve a given problem is called a program. In this part, the mechanisms for writing and executing programs in *Matlab will* be presented. We will then talk about tests and loops, starting with the introduction of comparison operators and logical operators.

1. General principle

The principle is simple: gather a series of *Matlab* commands in a file and execute them as a block. Everything will happen as if you were typing them as you go along in a *Matlab* session. It is strongly advised to proceed in this way by creating a programme file (M-file) because this allows you to easily recover the work done the day before.

The command files can have any name but must end with the .m extension (be careful however with certain characters which are forbidden: the blank, the + symbol,...). *Matlab* will not say this immediately but will send an error message on the first attempt to execute the file, saying that the file cannot be found).

2. Where should the order file be located?

The simplest is that it is in the current directory (i.e. the one where *Matlab was* launched). It can also be in any directory but referenced in the *Matlab* path variable. Type this command to see its contents, *Matlab* will show you all the accessible directories. It is generally advised to create your own directory or to use the default directory of *Matlab*. To find out the current directory just type the *pwd* command in the *Matlab* prompt.

The path can be modified with the *addpath* command. This command places the path to the file in the file which contains all default or declared paths, i.e. path, and is executed automatically at *Matlab* start up. Here is an example:

addpath   (genpath('C:\Documents   and   Settings\admin\Mes documents\MATLAB\Dossier'))

This command allows to add the new directory "Folder", created in the default directory of *Matlab which* is named MATLAB, to the access path.

Thus all the command files in the new "Folder" directory will be accessible from anywhere.

3. Comments and self-documentation

Anything after the % symbol will be considered a comment. It is also possible to self-document your order files.

4. Deleting the display

It is not necessary to display the results of all orders. For some orders (creation of large tables), this can be tedious.

You can therefore place the character; at the end of a command line to indicate to *Matlab* that it should not display the result.

5. Pause in execution

If the pause command is entered in a command file, the program will stop at this line until "Enter" or "Enter" is typed in the case of a QWERTY keyboard.

6. Verb mode

If you want *Matlab* to display the sequence of commands it is executing as it is being executed, just type :

>> echo on

To return to normal mode, simply press *echo off*. This mode can be used in combination with pause so that the programme displays a comment such as "Press any key to continue". Simply write the message in a comment :

echo on

pause % Press a key to continue!

echo off

7. Comparison operators and logics

Matlab uses the C language. First of all, let us note the following important point, inspired by the C language:

Matlab represents the logical constant "FALSE" by 0 and the constant "TRUE" by 1.

This is particularly useful, for example, when defining functions in pieces.

It is important to become familiar with logical operators. The first type of these operators allows you to compare values with each other.

Operator	Matlab syntax
Equal to	= =

Different from	~ =
Greater than	>
Greater than or equal to	>=
Less than	<
Less than or equal to	<=
Disclaimer	~
Or	|
And	&

For example, we want to compare two values with each other:

> > a=sin(2*pi);

> > b=cos(2*pi);

> > bool=(a>b)

bool=

0

> > a

a=

-2.4493e-016   % here a should equal 0, the accuracy is limited!

> > b

b=

1

Logic operators are interesting for building functions in pieces. Let's imagine that we want to define the following function: $f(x)=\begin{cases} \sin(x) & \text{si } x>0 \\ \sin(2x) & \text{sinon} \end{cases}$.

This is how to write the function:

>> f = inline('sin(x).*(x>0) + sin(2*x).*not(x>0)')

f =

    Inline function:

f(x) = sin(x).*(x>0) + sin(2*x).*not(x>0)

We add the two expressions sin x and sin 2x by weighting them by the logical condition defining their fields of validity. We can test that it works by representing the curve:

>> x=-2*ft:2*ft/100:2*ft;

>> plot(x,f(x))

It should be noted here that the use of the '==' operator is very risky when comparing numerical values. Indeed, as the precision of the computer is limited, it is preferable to use a difference condition as in the following code:

if abs(a-b) < eps % eps   is the machine accuracy (2.2204e-016)

bool=1;
else
bool=0;
end

It is also possible to link conditions between them by the operator 'and' (&) and 'or' (|).

These concepts will be useful in constructing the conditions that will be presented in the next sections.

Criterion on values: *find* function

We have seen how easy it is to apply a logical operator on a board. This returns an array containing 1's or 0's (logical values true or false) depending on whether the logical criterion is verified or not. This principle can be exploited to easily write a function defined in pieces, but it does not allow to extract or modify values according to a logical test. The *find* function can be used to do this.

The *find* function is useful to simply identify non-zero elements in a table, and by extension, to identify values verifying a given logical criterion.

indices = find(M)   %returns in the variable indices the list of indices in table M with non-zero elements.

index = find(logical operation on M)   %returns in the index variable the list of indices in table M verifying the logical operation.

For example:

> > x = [-1.2 0 3.1 6.2 -3.3 -2.1]

x =

    -1.2000   0   3.1000   6.2000   -3.3000   -2.1000

>> find(x) %The find function allows to identify the elements with non-zero values.

years =

    1   3   4   5   6

> > inds = find(x < 0) % allows   to find all the elements corresponding to a logical criterion :

inds =

    1   5   6

8. Inputs/outputs

a) Keyboard entry :

The user can enter information on the keyboard using the x=input(...) command.

>> X=input ('enter a value of x :')

enter a value of x : 5

X =

    5

b) Output to the screen

To display something on the screen, the user can use the disp command, which displays the content of a variable (string, vector, matrix...).

```
>> A=[1 2 3] ;
disp(A);
    1    2    3
```

9. Inspection instructions

The control instructions in Matlab are very similar to those in other programming languages.

a) if-elseif-else earrings

Conditions often intervene in a programme. The *if-elseif-else* loops are a programming structure which is very useful for reporting on this situation.

In pseudo-code, this can be summarised as follows:

```
if CONDITION1, TAKE ACTION1. % condition 1 met
otherwise and if CONDITION2, DO ACTION2. % condition 1 not fulfilled,
                                % but condition 2 met
otherwise, DO ACTION3     % conditions 1 and 2 not met
```

In *Matlab*, the previous pseudo-code becomes :

```
if CONDITION1
ACTION1;
elseif CONDITION2
ACTION2;
else
ACTION3;
end
```

If the condition is set to true, the instructions between the *if* and the *end will be* executed), otherwise they will not be (or if an *else* exists the instructions between the *else* and the *end* will be executed). If it is necessary to check several conditions instead of just one, *elseif* clauses can be used for each new condition, and at the end an *else* can be put in case no condition has been evaluated to true.

For example :

We receive an integer a, if it is odd negative, we make it positive. If it is odd positive, we add 1 to it. If it is even, we add 2 to its absolute value.

The following short function allows you to perform this transformation (note here the use of the modulo to determine if the integer is divisible by 2).

```
function b=transf_entity(a)
```

if a<0 &   mod(a,2) ~= 0 % mod   finds the rest of a division
b=-a;
elseif a>=0 & mod(a,2) ~= 0
b=a+1;
else
b=abs(a)+2;
end

If an instruction ends with a semicolon, then the value of the variable concerned will not be displayed, but if it ends with a comma or a line break, then the results will be displayed.

Remark

There is the predefined *solve* function in *Matlab* to find the roots of an equation (and much more). If we want to apply it to our example, just write :

>> solve('-2*x^2+x+3=0','x')

years =

-1

3/2

b) **Buckles for**

For loops are very useful in most mathematical applications (e.g. to perform a calculation on all the elements of a vector).

In *Matlab*, it is sometimes much more efficient to use the usual algebraic operators defined earlier (for example, the '.*'). In cases where it is considered possible to avoid the use of these loops, here is the pseudo-code prototype that translates them.

Increment = initial value

For increment=initial_value to final value

ACTION1...N

ADD 1 in increments

In *Matlab*, this pseudo-code becomes :

for i = 0:final_value

ACTION1;

ACTION2;

...

ACTION;

end

Note that the increment may be different from 1,

For example :

if one wants to calculate the squares of even numbers between 0 and 10 :

for i=0:2:10

square = i^2
end

c) Loops while

A *while* loop allows an operation to be repeated as long as a condition (criterion)
is not met. In pseudo-code, it can be schematised as follows:
As long as the CONDITION is TRUE
ACTION1...N
In *Matlab*, this type of loop is written as follows:
while CONDITION
ACTION1;
ACTION2;

...

ACTION;
end

This type of loop is very often used to converge an iteration to a desired value
whose accuracy is set by a convergence test.

For example :

We want to find the number of positive integers needed to have a sum greater
than 100. This could be done in the following way:
function n=full_number
n=0;   % initialization of values
sum=0;
while sum < 100
n=n+1; % iteration of n
sum=sum+n; % new sum
end

d) Switch loops

Switch loops are sometimes used to replace *if-elseif-else* loops, especially in the
case of menus. The *switch* loop executes groups of instructions based on the
value of a variable or expression. Each group has a *box* clause associated with it
that defines whether or not the group should be executed based on whether the
value of the *box is* equal to the evaluation results of the *switch* expression. If all
the *boxes* have not been accepted, it is possible to add *another clause box* which
will be executed only if no *box* is executed.
The prototype of this type of loop in pseudo-code is the following:
Determine CAS
CASE chosen is CAS1
ACTION1
CAS chosen is CAS2

ACTION2
OTHERWISE
ACTION3
In *Matlab*, the following code is obtained:
switch (CAS)
box {CAS1}.
ACTION1
box {CAS2}
ACTION2
otherwise
ACTION3
end
For example :
We want to make a simple calculator in *Matlab*, to determine the exponential or logarithm in base e of a number entered by the user.
A simple way to make the program interactive would be to use the following script:
operation=input('Operation: (1) exp; (2) log ? ');
number=input('Value: ');
switch operation
box 1
b=exp(number)
box 2
b= log(number)
otherwise
disp('wrong choice -- operation')
end
With the following output (for example) :
> > quick_calculation
Operation: (1) exp; (2) log ? 1
Value: 0.5
b =
1.6487

Chapter 6: Applications of numerical methods with Matlab

1. Introduction :

Numerical analysis is used to find approximations to difficult problems such as solving non-linear equations, integration involving complex expressions. It is applied to a wide variety of disciplines such as all areas of engineering, computer science, education, geology, meteorology, and many others. Years ago, high-speed computers did not exist, so manual calculation required a lot of time and laborious work. But now that computers have become indispensable for research work in science, engineering and other fields, numerical analysis has become a much easier and more enjoyable task.

2. Resolution of linear systems using Matlab software: Gauss Pivot method (direct method)

The Gauss pivot method is a direct method of linear system resolution which allows a system to be transformed into another equivalent scaled system. The resulting system is solved using a pullup algorithm.

Principle

We try to solve the following system of n equations with n unknowns $x_1, x_2, ..., x_n$:

$$\begin{cases} a_{11}x_1 + a_{12}x_2 + ... + a_{1n}x_n = b_1 \\ a_{21}x_1 + a_{22}x_2 + ... + a_{2n}x_n = b_2 \\ \quad\quad\quad\vdots \\ a_{n1}x_1 + a_{n2}x_2 + ... + a_{nn}x_n = b_n \end{cases}$$

From the matrix point of view, we have   **Ax=b**

With

$$\begin{bmatrix} a_{11} & a_{12} & ... & a_{1n} \\ a_{21} & a_{22} & ... & a_{2n} \\ ... & ... & ... & ... \\ a_{n1} & a_{n2} & ... & a_{nn} \end{bmatrix} \begin{bmatrix} x_1 \\ x_2 \\ ... \\ x_n \end{bmatrix} = \begin{bmatrix} b_1 \\ b_2 \\ ... \\ b_n \end{bmatrix}$$

The data of the linear system are:

- real or complex coefficients a_{ij} for i=1,...,n and j=1,...,,p (n and p are two known integers).

- the second member of the system, consisting of real or complex numbers $b_i (i=1,...,n)$, $L_i (i=1,...,n)$ designates the i-th line of the system (S).

- the unknowns to be determined are $x_j (j=1,...,p)$.

The system is said to be square when n=p . This is the case when there are as many equations as there are unknowns.

The system is said to be homogeneous when the second member is null $(b_i =0,i=1,...,n)$.

It can be noted that a homogeneous linear system admits at least the null solution.

$(x_i =0,\forall i=1,...,n)$ (which is not necessarily the only one).

When all the coefficients "below the diagonal" of a linear system are zero . i.e:

$$i>j \Rightarrow a_{ij}=0$$

The system is said to be staggered.

   i.   *the Gauss pivot method: Triangularisation*

$$k=1,...,n-1 \begin{cases} a_{ij}^{(k+1)} =a_{ij}^{(k)} & i=1,...,k \quad j=1,...,n \\ a_{ij}^{(k+1)} =0 & i=k+1,...,n \quad j=1,...,k \\ a_{ij}^{(k+1)} =a_{ij}^{(k)} -\dfrac{a_{ik}^{(k)}a_{kj}^{(k)}}{a_{kk}^{(k)}} & i=k+1,...,n \quad j=k+1,...,n \\ b_i^{(k+1)} =b_i^{(k)} & i=1,...k \\ b_i^{(k+1)} =b_i^{(k)} -\dfrac{a_{ik}^{(k)}b_k^{(k)}}{a_{kk}^{(k)}} & i=k+1,...,n \end{cases}$$

Let U be the staggered matrix of the system, then we have

$$U=\left(u_{ij}\right)_{1\le i,j\le n} =\left(a_{ij}^{(n)}\right)_{1\le i,j\le n}$$

   ii.   Ascent and resolution

Now that the matrix A of the linear system is scaled, the triangular system must be solved:

$$Ux=b(n)$$

Since b(n), as we recall, is the second staggered member, it has undergone the same operations as the U staggered matrix.

An ascent algorithm for the Ux=b(n) system   is then used:

$$\begin{cases} x_n =\dfrac{y_n}{u_{nn}} =\dfrac{y_n}{a_{nn}^{(n)}}; \\ x_i =\dfrac{1}{u_{ii}}\left(y_i -\displaystyle\sum_{j=i+1}^{n} u_{ij}x_j\right) =\dfrac{1}{a_{ii}^{(n)}}\left(y_i -\displaystyle\sum_{j=i+1}^{n} a_{ij}^{(n)}x_j\right) \forall i=n+1,n-2,...,1 \end{cases}$$

   iii.   Example of a resolution

Consider the following system:

$$\begin{cases} x_1 + 2x_2 + 3x_3 = 2 \ \ L_1 \\ x_1 + 3x_2 - 2x_3 = -1 \ \ L_2 \\ 3x_1 + 5x_2 + 8x_3 = 8 \ \ L_3 \end{cases}$$

with

$$A = \begin{pmatrix} 1 & 2 & 2 \\ 1 & 3 & -2 \\ 3 & 5 & 8 \end{pmatrix} ; x = \begin{pmatrix} x_1 \\ x_2 \\ x_3 \end{pmatrix} ; b = \begin{pmatrix} 2 \\ -1 \\ 8 \end{pmatrix}$$

First step of the Gauss pivot to eliminate variables x_1 in the lines L_2 et L_3 :

$$\begin{cases} x_1 + 2x_2 + 2x_3 & = 2 \quad L_1 \\ x_2 - 4x_3 & = -3 \quad L_2 \leftarrow L_2 - L_1 \\ -x_2 + 2x_3 & = 2 \quad L_3 \leftarrow L_3 - 3L_1 \end{cases}$$

Second step of the Gauss pivot to eliminate variables x_2 in the line L_3 :

$$\begin{cases} x_1 + 2x_2 + 2x_3 & = 2 \quad L_1 \\ x_2 - 4x_3 & = -3 \quad L_2 \\ -2x_3 & = -1 \quad L_3 \leftarrow L_3 + L_2 \end{cases}$$

By reassembling the system, system solution x is easily achieved:

$$x = \begin{pmatrix} 3 \\ -1 \\ 1/2 \end{pmatrix}$$

iv.   Matlab code implementing the Gauss method

```
clear all
close
size=input(' Matrix   size:   ');
for   t=1:size
for p= 1:size
 str=sprintf('Enter the element (%d,%d) of the martice A: ',t,p);
a(t,p)=input(str);
end
end
for t=1:size
for p=1:size
str=sprintf('Enter the element (%d,%d) of martice B: ',t,p);
b(t,p)=input(str);
end
end
disp(a)
disp(b)
A=[a,b]
```

```
n=size(A,1);
for k=1:n-1
for i=k+1:n
     w=A(i,k)/A(k,k)
for j=k:n+1
        A(i,j)=A(i,j)-w*A(k,j)
end
end
end
A
for i=n:-1:1
   s=0;
for j=i+1:n
     s=s+A(i,j)*x(j);
end
   x(i)=(A(i,n+1)-s)/A(i,i);
end
x
```

According to the Matlab code. We obtain solution x from the following system:

x =

   3.0000   -1.0000   0.5000

3. Solving non-linear equations (Newton-Raphson method)

a) The Newton-Raphson method

The Newton-Raphson method consists in finding the value x which will cancel the function f(x).

The Newton-Raphson method makes it possible to iteratively approximate the x-value by means of the following relationship:

$$x_{n+1} = x_n - \frac{f(x_n)}{f'(x_n)}$$

If then $|x_n - x_{n-1}| < \varepsilon$ x_n is the result of the root estimate.

where ε represent approximation errors characterising the quality of the digital solution.

This stopping criterion has the advantage of avoiding a possible division by 0. In all iterative methods, it is necessary to choose the initial value to avoid a divergence of the solution x_0. This can be obtained graphically.

Example:

We propose to apply this method to the search for the roots of the following non-linear function:

$$f(x)=e^x-2\cos(x)$$

The first step is to draw the representative curve of this function using the program below ' NewtonRaphson.m':

```
% study of the function:
%f(x)=exp(x)-2*cos(x)
x=-1:0.1:1;
f=exp(x)-2*cos(x);
plot(x,f);
grid on;
title('fonctin: f(x)=exp(x)-2*cos(x)');
```

After running the programme, the curve is shown in the figure below.
 According to this curve, it makes sense to choose an x0 = 0.5; because f(x0) is close to zero, in order to have a fast convergence. The derivative function f'(x) has as expression:

$$f'(x)=e^x+2\sin(x).$$

The calculation of sera x_1 :

$$x_1=x_0-\frac{f(x_0)}{f'(x_0)}=0.5-\frac{-0.1064}{2.6075}$$

$$x_1=0.5408$$

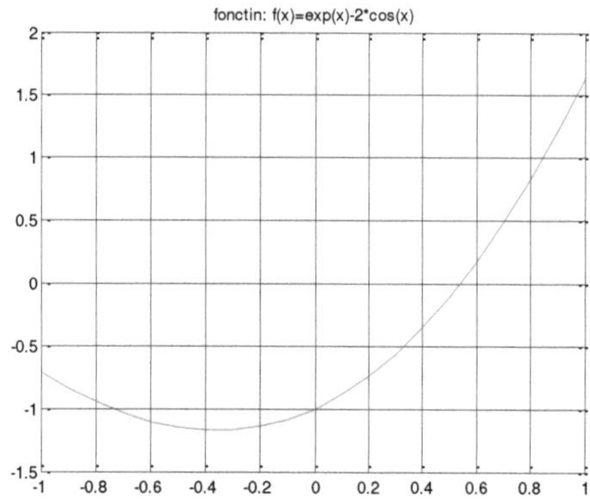

Figure 1:Location of the x0 value where $f(x_0)\cong0$

To search for the solution of $f(x)$, you can add a few lines to the previous programme 'NewtonRaphson.m':

```matlab
% study of the function:
%f(x)=exp(x)-2*cos(x)
x=-1:0.1:1;
f=exp(x)-2*cos(x);
figure(1);
plot(x,f);
grid on;
title('fonctin: f(x)=exp(x)-2*cos(x)');
clear all;
clc;
x(1)=input('Give initial value x(1):    \n');
e=1e-10;
n=5000;
for i=2:n
    f=exp(x(i-1))-2*cos(x(i-1));
    diff=exp(x(i-1))+2*sin(x(i-1));
    x(i)=x(i-1)-f/diff;
if abs(x(i)-x(i-1))< =e
 xp=x(i);
 fprintf('xp=%f\n',x(i));
station wagon
end
end
for j=1:i;
figure(2);
plot(j,x(j),'*r',j,x(j));
xlabel('Number of iterations');
title('Convergence of the solution: New.-Raph. method');
disp('The successive values of x(i) are:');
x'
end;
```

According to the Matlab code. You get :

xp=0.539785

The successive values of x(i) are :

years =

    0.5000
    0.5408
    0.5398

0.5398

0.5398

b) Dichotomy method:

i. **Principle:** Consider a function f continuous over an interval [a,b]. It is assumed that f admits one and only one root α in $]a,b[$ and $f(a).f(b)<0$. We note

$$c=\frac{a+b}{2}$$

the middle of the interval.

1) If $f(c)=0$, it is the root of f and the problem is solved.

2) If $f(c)\neq0$, we look at the sign of $f(a).f(b)$.

(a) If $f(a).f(c)<0$, then $\alpha\in]a,c]$

(b) If $f(c).f(b)<0$ then $\alpha\in]c,b]$

The process is repeated by taking the interval $[a,c]$ instead of th$[a,b]$ $(a_n),(b_n),(c_n)$, such $a_0=a, b_0=b$ and such as for everything $n\geq0$.

(1) $c_n=\dfrac{a_n+b_n}{2}$

(2) If then $f(c_n).f(b_n)<0$ and $a_{n+1}=c_n$ $b_{n+1}=b_n$

(3) If $f(c_n).f(a_n)<0$ then and $a_{n+1}=a_n$ $b_{n+1}=c_n$

ii. The above algorithm is called the dichotomy algorithm.

1. If f(a)=0 print the solution is a . If f(b)=0 print solution is b, go to 10.
2. If f(b)*f(a)>0, print (no change in sign), go to 10.
3. Lay N=1.
4. As long as N<=N0, do steps 5 to 8.
5. Poser $p=\dfrac{a+b}{2}$
6. If f(p)=0 or $\dfrac{b-a}{2}\leq\epsilon$ print p, go to 10.
7. Laying N=N+1
8. If f(a)*f(p)>0, then lay a=p, otherwise lay b=p.
9. Print after N0 iterations the approximation obtained is p and the maximum error is $\dfrac{b-a}{2}$
10. End

iii.   Study of convergence.

Theorem 2. Let f be a continuous function on [a, b]; verifying and be $\alpha \in [a,b]$ $f(a).(b)<0$ the only solution to the equation f (x) = 0. If the dichotomy algorithm reaches step n then we have the estimate :

$$|\alpha - c_n| \le \frac{b-a}{2^n + 1}$$

Therefore, the following (c_n) converges towards α . This is also true if $(c_n) = \alpha$

Demonstration: Just note that at each iteration, the interval is divided by two.

iv.   Stop test.

In order for the value of c_n the continuation to the n-th iteration to be a value that is close to the $\varepsilon > 0$ α nearest value, it is sufficient for n to check:

$$\frac{b-a}{2^n + 1} \le \varepsilon$$

We then have :

$$|\alpha - c_n| \le \frac{b-a}{2^n + 1} \le \varepsilon$$

This makes it $n_0 \in N$ possible to calculate in advance the maximum number of iterations to ensure accuracy ε .

$$\frac{b-a}{2^n + 1} \le \varepsilon \Leftrightarrow \frac{b-a}{\varepsilon} \le 2^n + 1 \Leftrightarrow n \ge \frac{\log \dfrac{b-a}{\varepsilon}}{\log(2)} - 1$$

c) Fixed point method

This method allows to solve numerically equations of the type g(x) = x, i.e. to determine the fixed points of g.

It is based on the use of a sequence defined by a recurrence $x_{n+1} = g(x_n)$, **Indeed,** if such a sequence admits a limit $x, x_n \to x$ then $x_{n+1} \to x$ and if g is continuous, by passing to the limit one obtains g(x) = x : the limit of such a sequence is necessarily one of the fixed points of g.

The difficulty is to ensure that the sequence converges...and towards the "right" fixed point: a sequence $\qquad x_{n+1} = f(x_n)$ may not converge, or may converge towards another fixed point than the one sought.

i.   Proposal

or I an interval of R and $g : I \to R$ derivable. Such as :

➢ There are s in I as g(s)=s;

- I is stable per g (i.e) $g(I) \subset I$.
- It exists a< I such that for every x of I , .

So if we take x_0 any element of I and define for all n $x_{n+1} = g(x_n)$, then converge to s x_0.

ii.   Fixed point algorithm

Goal: Find a solution of g(x)=x

Entrance fees : An initial approximation p0

 ε(the desired precision)

NO the maximum number of iterations

Output: Approximate value of p or in failure message

Step 1: Laying N=1

Step2: While N≤N0, do steps 3 to 6

Step 3: lay p=g(p0)

Step 4: If $|$ p-p0 $| \leq \varepsilon$

   Then print p

   Go to step 8

Step 7: Print (method failed after N0 iterations)

Step8 : End

Exercise 1
___

Test and understand the following two lines

- A=[1   2   −1   1   ;   −1   1   0   3]

- **find(A>0)**

Answers to Exercise 1
___

% Matlab's prompt is typed in

>> A=[1 2 -1 1; -1 1 0 3]

A =

   1   2   -1   1

  -1   1   0   3

The previous command allows to create a table (matrix) type variable with two

% rows and four columns. The first line contains the terms specified by the list

% 1 2 -1 1 which are separated by a blank, while the terms in the second line

% start after the semicolon separating lines and are defined by the list -1 1 0 3.

% Matlab's prompt is typed in

find(A>0)

years =

   1

   3

   4

   7

   8

% The *find* command allows you to find the indices of the terms in a table according to the criterion

% specified in brackets. Here the criterion is A>0 which means that we want the terms

% of Table A that are strictly positive. The numbering with a single index adopted by

% Matlab is such that the terms are numbered in columns from top to bottom and from left to right to

% right. The first term of A is therefore 1, the second is -1, the third is 2, ...,
the
% seventh and 1 and the eighth is 3. The *find* command produces as a result
the list
% 1 3 4 7 8 which represents the indices of the terms (not the terms) in the
matrix A that
% meet the criterion.

Exercise 2

We note and u,v **the following vectors :** w $u=\begin{bmatrix} 1 & -1 & 2 \end{bmatrix}^t$ $v=\begin{bmatrix} 10 & -1 & 3 \end{bmatrix}^t$, $w=\begin{bmatrix} 5 & -1 & 4 \end{bmatrix}^t$

- **Calculate** $a=3u$, $b=2u-v+5w$, $c=w-4v$.

Answers to Exercise 2

1.% You type in the Matlab prompt
>> u=[1 -1 2].'

u =

    1

   -1

    2

Note the presence of the symbol . ' at the end of the instruction which means
the transposed according to the Matlab syntax.
% Then type in the Matlab prompt
>> v=[10 -1 3].'

v =

   10

   -1

    3

>> w=[5 -1 4].'

w =

    5

   -1

    4

% To calculate 3u, type in the Matlab prompt
>>a= 3*u

years =

    3

   -3

6
The result is therefore written in mathematical notation $[3\ -3\ 6]^t$

% To calculate $2u-v+5w$, type in the Matlab prompt

>>b= 2*u-v+5*w

years =

    17
    -6
    21

% The result is therefore $[17\ \ -6\ \ 2]^t$. Note that it is necessary to put * which represents the multiplication operation and that the calculation cannot be made using the mathematical   notation 2u-v+5w which would produce an error message.

% To calculate $w-4v$ type in the Matlab prompt

>> c=w-4*v

c =

   -35
     3
    -8

Exercise 3

- **We note u and v complex numbers: u =11-7i , v=-1+3i .**

- **Calculate the u and v modules, the products $u\bar{v}+\bar{u}v$, the real part and the imaginary part. u^3+v^2**

Answers to Exercise 3

---

1. To calculate u =11-7i , the Matlab prompt (with the precaution indicated at i) is used to type in

>> u=11-7i

u =

11.0000 - 7.0000i

To assign the complex value -1+3i to v , in the Matlab prompt type the instruction

Next % of the total

>> v=-1+3i

v =

-1.0000 + 3.0000i

2. The modules of u and v are calculated by the commands abs(u) and abs(b), where the function

% Thus, we obtain

>> abs(u)

years =

13.0384

>> abs(v)

years =

3.1623

% The conjugate of a complex number is calculated in Matlab with the command conj.

To calculate the expression $u\bar{v}+\bar{u}v$, type in the Matlab prompt

>> u*conj(v)+conj(u)*v

years =

-64

% To calculate the real and imaginary parts of u^3+v^2, type in the Matlab prompt

% of orders

>> real(u^3+v^2)

years =

-294

% and

>> imag(u^3+v^2)

years =

-2204

Exercise 4

We lay

$$A=\begin{bmatrix} 1 & -1 & 7 \\ -4 & 2 & 11 \\ 8 & 0 & 3 \end{bmatrix},\ B=\begin{bmatrix} 3 & -2 & -1 \\ 7 & 8 & 6 \\ 5 & 1 & 3 \end{bmatrix}$$

- **What do the following instructions do? $3*A$; $A.*B$; $A./B$; $\cos(A)$; $\exp(B)$.**

Answers to Exercise 4

The answer to the question asked in this exercise is obtained by the following instructions:

>> A=[1 -1 7; -4 2 11; 8 0 3]

A =
     1   -1   7
    -4   2   11
     8   0   3
>> B=[3 -2 -1; 7 8 6; 5 1 3]
B =
     3   -2   -1
     7   8   6
     5   1   3
>> 3*A
years =
     3   -3   21
   -12   6   33
    24   0   9
>> A.*B
years =
     3   2   -7
   -28   16   66
    40   0   9
>> A./B
years =
    0.333333333333333   0.500000000000000 -7.000000000000000
   -0.571428571428571   0.2500000000000   00 1.833333333333333
    1.6000000000000   00 0   1.000000000000000
>> cos(A)
years =
    0.5403   0.5403   0.7539
   -0.6536   -0.4161   0.0044
   -0.1455   1.0000   -0.9900
  %
  >> exp(B)
  years =
  1.0e+03 *
    0.0201   0.0001   0.0004
    1.0966   2.9810   0.4034
    0.1484   0.0027   0.0201

Exercise 5

1. Create a vector of 11 components containing the numbers $-5, -4, \ldots, 4, 5$

2. Create a vector of 1001 components containing the numbers
$-500, -499, -498, ..., 499, 500$

3. Create a vector u **containing 10 values between and** π 0 **separated by a constant increment.**

Answers to Exercise 5.

1.% The command to be used is *linspace*. We then write in the Matlab prompt
>> v1=space(-5,5,11)
v1 =
   -5   -4   -3   -2   -1   0   1   2   3   4   5
2.% We then write in Matlab's invitation.
>> v2=space(-500,500,1001) ;
3. % Just type
>> v3=space(0,ft,10)
 Columns 1 through 9

Exercise 6

- **Write a Script File or function called polaire.m that converts the cartesian coordinates of a point to polar coordinates.**

- **Convert the following Cartesian coordinates: (0,1)**

Answers to Exercise 6

---

function [radius,theta]=polar(x,y)
radius=sqrt(x^2+y^2);
theta=atan(y/x);
end

When calling our polar function to calculate the two polar coordinates of a point defined for example by its two Cartesian coordinates (0,1), it should be done in the following form:
>> [radius,theta]=polar(0,1)
radius =   1
theta =   1.5708

Exercise 7

---

1. Write a Script File for the function $f(x)=\dfrac{x^5-3}{\sqrt{x^2+1}}$

2. Test the function on a few values, for example $f(1)=-1.4142$, $f(0)=-3$.

3. Create an x-table of abscissae from -5 to 5 and containing 100 points.

4. Represent the function f at points xi, with the command plot (x,f(x))

Answers to exercise 7

1. The following script can be used to define the function f :

```
function [fdex]=function_f(x)
fdex=(x^5-3)/sqrt(x^2+1);
end
```

2. The function can be tested with the commands

```
>> [fdex]=function_f(1)
fdex = -1.4142
>> [fdex]=function_f(0)
fdex =   -3
```

3. The table is created by the following command

```
>>x=space(-5,5,100) ;
```

4. In order to graphically represent the function f at the points xi of the table x created in the previous question, it is sufficient to transform the arithmetic operations that appear in the Script into forward operations that have the possibility to operate on tables. Here is the relevant transformation that must be carried out in the Script that defines the function f.

```
function [fdex]=function_f(x)
fdex=(x.^5-3)./sqrt(x.^2+1);
end
```

Finally, the function can be traced using the following commands, which preferably should be written in a script that calls function_f and asks *Matlab to* make the graphical representation (it can be called function_trace):

```
%trace_of_function
clear all;
close all;
x=linspace(-5,5,100);
y]=function_f(x);
plot(x,y)
```

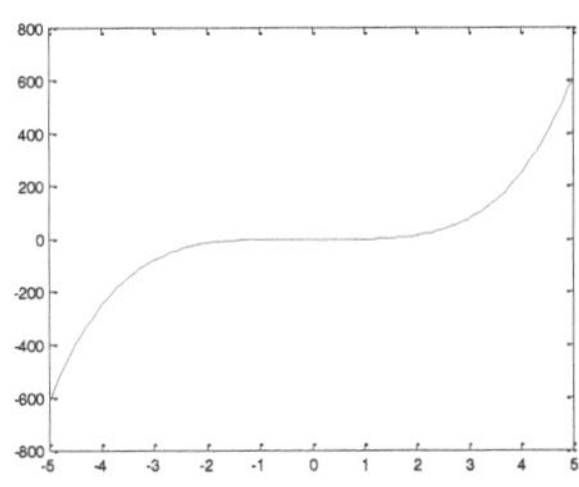

Exercise 8

Write a script for the function: $f(x) = \exp(\sin(x))$ **on th** e $[-\pi/2, \pi/2]$.

1. Calculate $f(0)$, and $f(\pi/4)$ $f(1)$.

2. Plot the function on $f(x)$ **red interval** $[-\pi/2, \pi/2]$, **name the x and y axes and give the curve a title.**

3. Calculate the maximum of $f(x)$ **over the interval** $[-\pi/2, \pi/2]$

Answers to exercise 8

1. The Script defining function f is then :
```
function [y]=ex3_function(x)
y=exp(sin(x));
end
```

2.   >> [y]=ex3_function (0)

y =

   1

>> [y]=ex3_function (ft/4)

y =

   2.0281

>> [y]=ex3_function (1)

y =

   2.3198

3. The following script is used to plot the curve of the f function over the interval $[-\pi/2, \pi/2]$
```
clear all;
close all;
x=space(-ft/2,ft/2,100);
y]=ex3_function(x);
plot(x,y, 'r-')
xlabel('x')
ylabel('f(x)')
title('Curve of the function f(x)=exp(sin(x))')
```

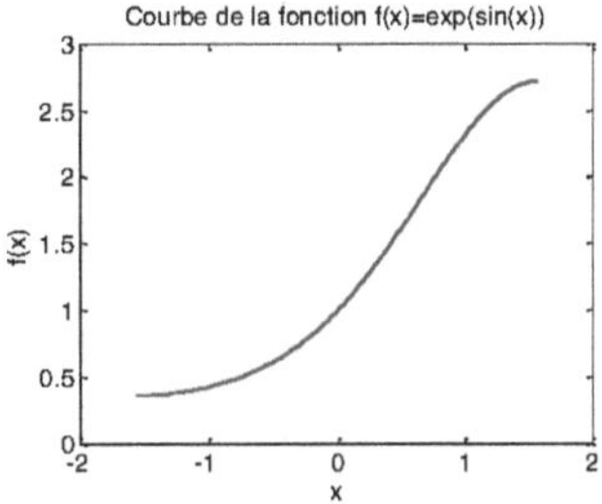

3. To calculate the maximum value taken by the function $f(x)$ on the interval in an approximate way, $[-\pi/2, \pi/2]$ just type the following command:

>> max(y)

years =

   2.7183

Financial year 9

Using the *surf* and *mesh* command, draw the $[-2,2]\times[-3,3]$ surface on the plane area that corresponds to the following Cartesian equation.
$z=e^{-x^2-y^2}$.

Corrected for the financial year 9

To draw the surface $(x,y)\mapsto z=e^{-x^2-y^2}$, you just have to create two tables: one with the xi abscissa on the domain $[-2,2]$, the other with the yj ordinate on the domain an $[-3,3]$ then calculate the zij dimension corresponding to each pair (xi,yj) *surf* or *mesh* command.

All these operations are grouped together in the following script:

```
clear all;
close all;
N=60;
x=(linspace(-2,2,N))'*ones(1,N);
y=ones(N,1)*space(-3,3,N);
z=exp(-x.^2-y.^2);
mesh(x,y,z)
axis([-2 2 -3 3 0 1]);
box;
```

The following graph is then obtained:

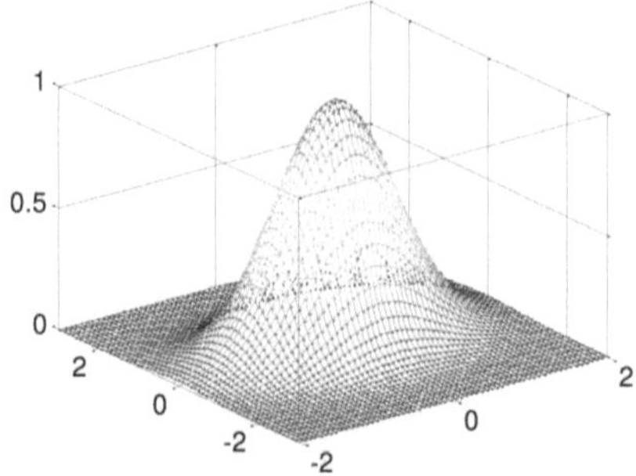

By substituting the *surf* command for the *mesh* command, the result becomes

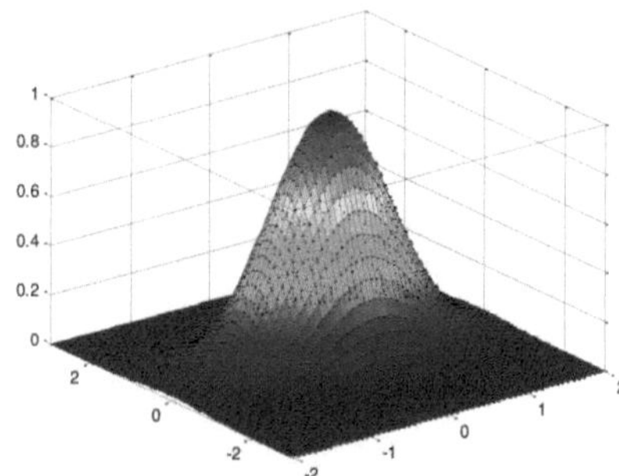

Note here the trick which allows to transform the table of abscissae into a matrix containing all the abscissae of the points which discretize the domain $[-2,2]\times[-3,3]$. This matrix admits identical lines. Another transformation makes it possible to recover a matrix of ordinates with this time the columns which are identical. The calculation of z can then be performed in block using the expression exp(-x.^2-y.^2) constant per row of the x matrix and constant per column of the y matrix.

Exercise₁10

Translate the following GCD algorithm into Matlab language:
a,b positive integers
what to $a\neq b$ **do**
 if $a>b$ **then** $a\leftarrow a-b$
 otherwise $b\leftarrow b-a$
fine as well as
 $PGCD\leftarrow a$

Answers to Exercise 10

In order to translate the GCD algorithm considered in this exercise into Matlab language, we need the control structures, in this case the *while* loop and the *if-else-end* test. We propose the following M-file for the program translating this algorithm:

```matlab
clear all;
close all;
a=input('Enter the positive integer a   );
b=input('Enter positive integer b   );
a0=a;
b0=b;
while a~=b
 yew a>b
      a=a-b;
 else
      b=b-a;
 end
end
str=['The largest common divisor of ' num2str(a0) ' and ' num2str(b0) ' is '
num2str(a)];
disp(str);
```

*Auxiliary variables a0 and b0 are used to store the initial values of a and b which are changed in the *while loop and* therefore do not retain their input values at the output of this loop. They are actually overwritten in lines 9 and 11.

```
Enter the positive integer a    8
Enter the positive integer b    6
The largest common divisor of 8 and 6 is 2
```

Exercise 12

Write the function vec2col.m which transforms any vector (line or column) passed as an argument into a column vector. An error processing will test that the variable passed to the function is indeed a vector and not a matrix (use the size command).

Answers to exercise 12

The following M-file type function is offered:

```matlab
function [y]=vect2col(x)
n=size(x);
n1=n(1);
n2=n(2);
if n1==1
```

```
   y=x. ';
elseif n2==1
 y=x;
else
 error=['the input variable is not a row or column vector'];
 display(error)
end
```

It can be tested with the controls

```
>> vect2col([1 1 1])
years =
    1
    1
    1
>> vect2col([1; 1; 1])
years =
    1
    1
    1
>> vect2col([1 1; 1 2])
error =
the input variable is not a row or column vector
```

Exercise 13

Write a script that allows you to transform Cartesian coordinates (x,y,z) **into cylindrical** (r,θ,z) (ρ,θ,φ) **or spherical coordinates, depending on your choice.**

Corrected for the financial year 13

An example of a script responding to the statement is given below. Note that the cylindrical coordinates are output in the order: (r,θ,z) and the spherical coordinates in the order (r,θ,φ) .

```
function [a,b,c]=transformation(x,y,z,choice)
switch choice
 cylindrical box
 a=sqrt(x^2+y^2);
 b=atan(y/x);
     c=z;
 spherical' box
```

```
        a=sqrt(x^2+y^2+z^2);
        b=atan(y/x);
        c=atan(sqrt(x^2+y^2)/z);
 otherwise
 display('You did not specify the nature of the transformation')
end
end
```

Examples of use :
```
>> [a,b,c]=transformation(1,1,1,'cylindrical')
a =
    1.4142
b =
    0.7854
c =
    1
%
>> [a,b,c]=transformation(2,3,4, 'spherical')
a =
    5.3852
b =
    0.9828
c =
    0.7336
```
With *Matlab* you have four commands that allow you to transform Cartesian coordinates into cylindrical coordinates or Cartesian coordinates into spherical coordinates, as well as their inverses.
```
theta,rho,z]=cart2pol(x,y,z) % catesian to cylindrical transformation
x,y,z]=pol2cart(theta,rho,z) % cylindrical to cartesian transformation
theta,phi,r]=cart2pol(x,y,z) % catesian to spherical transformations
x,y,z]=sph2cart(theta,phi,r) % spherical transformation into catesians
```

Attention:
* Here all angles are calculated in radians (*Matlab* uses this unit by default).
* *Matlab* outputs cylindrical coordinates in the order (θ,r,z) and spherical coordinates in the order (θ,φ,r).

References

1. Nicolas Hudon. Initiation to Matlab, (nicolas.hudon@polymtl.ca), URCPC, Ecole Polytechnique de Montréal, 22 January 2004

2. Marie Postel. Introduction to Matlab software, Revised version September 2004. Jacques-Louis Lions Laboratory, Pierre and Marie Curie University.

3. Alfio Quarteroni, Fausto Saleri, Paola Gervasio. Scientific Calculus; Lectures, corrected exercises and illustrations in MATLAB and Octave. Springer-Verlag, Italy 2010.

4. Baba Hamid Fatima Zohra. Scientific Calculus Applied to Civil Engineering under Matlab, Course. University of Science and Technology of Oran Mohamd Boudiaf

Printed by Books on Demand GmbH, Norderstedt / Germany